Front Cover: "Doors to Nowhere" by Wally Gilbert, 2015.

Back Cover: "Pearls of Passion" by Inna Timokhina, 2016.

Wally Gilbert and INKA Collaborative

Copyright Notice: Copyright ©2017 by Wally Gilbert

An Exhibition

at

START

September 13th to 17th, 2017

Saatchi Gallery
London, England

Short Profile of the "Wally Gilbert and INKA Collaborative"

WALLY GILBERT had a long international career as a scientist, working in Molecular Biology on genes and DNA. He was awarded a Nobel Prize in Chemistry in 1980 for solving the mystery of DNA sequencing. Those discoveries drove the development of Biology as a gene-based science and led to the working out of the Human Genome program and the current understanding of all organisms. For the last fifteen years Gilbert has been working in Digital Art.

Inna Timokhina (aka INKA) is a scientist and an inventor. She received a Ph.D. in Molecular Biology from Cornell University and the Sloan-Kettering Cancer Center, and Wally Gilbert's work was a great inspiration for her. Prior to her studies in Molecular Biology, she received a formal education in visual arts in Russia. After spending more than a decade as a molecular scientist, Inna's passion for art re-emerged, and she has worked as an internationally exhibited artist for the past years.

In 2015 Wally and Inna met in person during Art Basel Miami and discovered that they shared a passion for abstract art. They formed a 2-artist collaborative, showcasing how their passion for discovery continues in art. "Wally Gilbert and INKA Collaborative" invites the viewer to a journey of discovery of the parallel worlds that they envision.

The center pieces of their exhibition at START are two large artworks: Wally Gilbert's "Doors to Nowhere" and Inna Timokhina's "Space–Time".

Catalogue of Images

By Inna Timokhina

Space–Time	10
Pearls of Passion	11
Jazz Me Up!	12
Gorgona Medusa	13
Acquamour	14
Cosmic Rendezvous	15
Fire Lotus	16

By Wally Gilbert

Doors to Nowhere	17
Torn Building Towers	18
Youth Day – Krakow	19
Broken City	20
Broken City #II	21
High Water – New York	22
Sequences Forever	23
Multiply Diptych	24

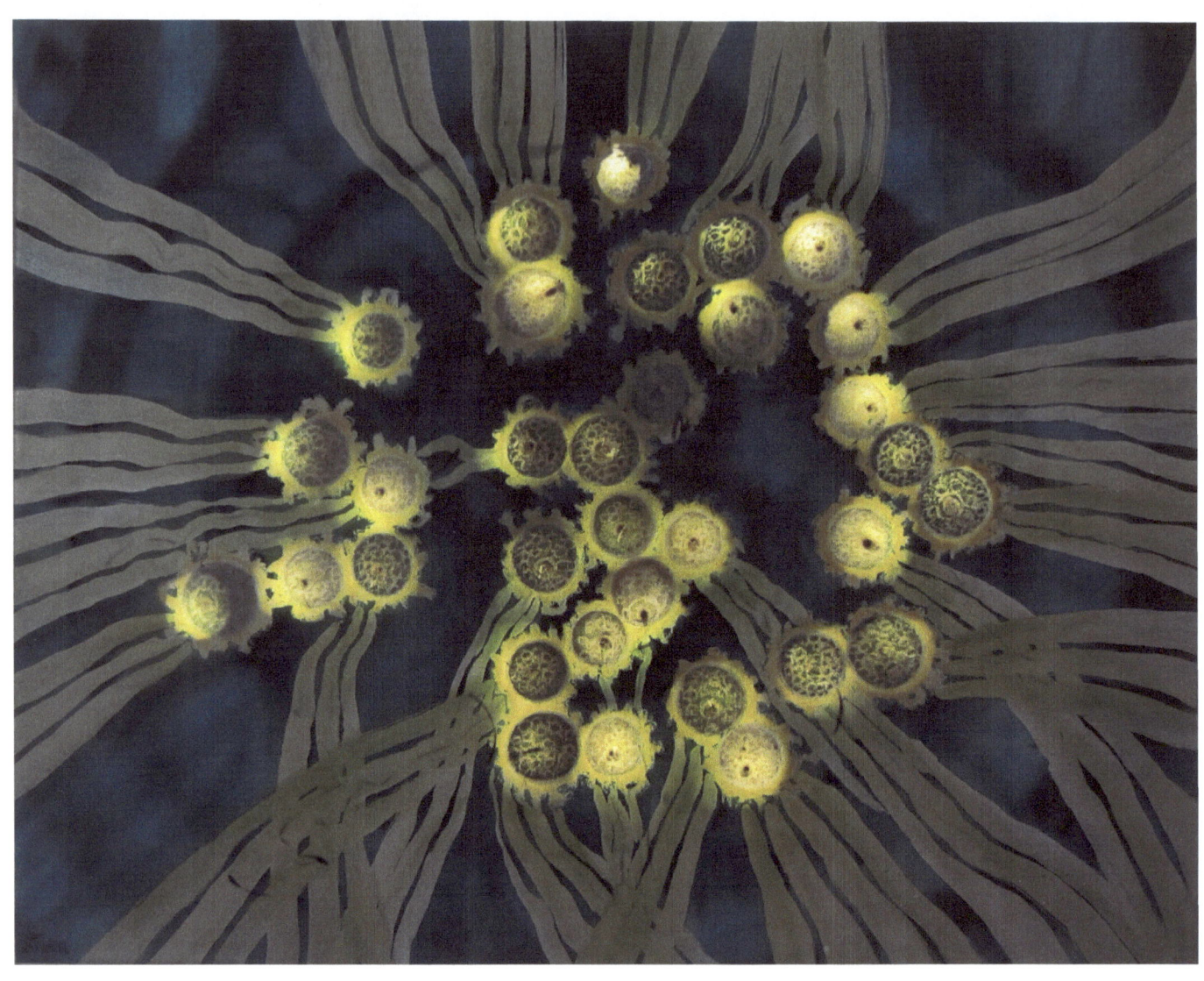

Space—Time

by Inna Timokhina, 2017, 100 cm x 125 cm,
Mixed Media on Plexiglass

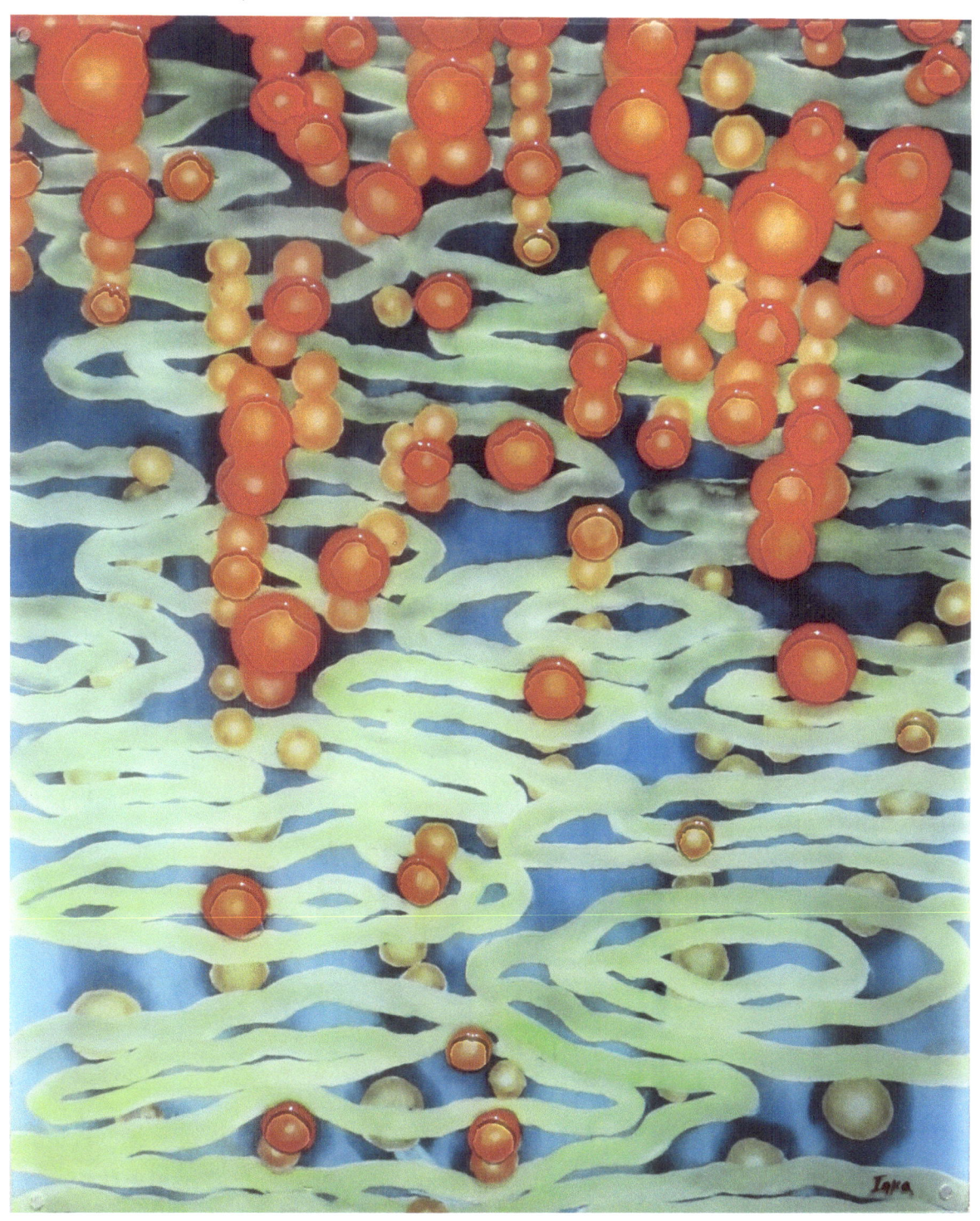

Pearls of Passion

by Inna Timokhina, 2016, 100 cm x 80 cm,
Mixed Media on Plexiglass

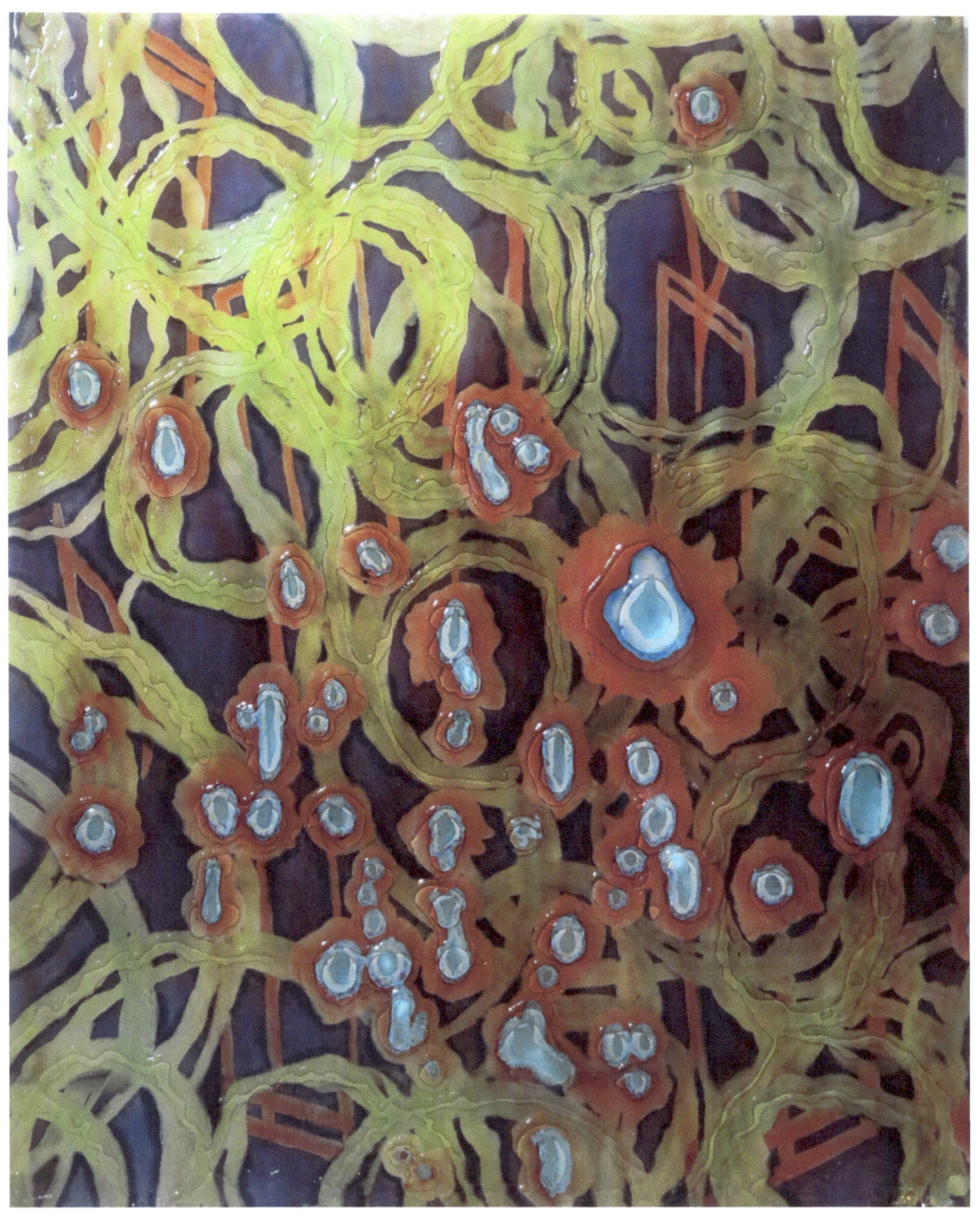

Jazz Me Up!

by Inna Timokhina, 2016, 100 cm x 80 cm,
Mixed Media on Plexiglass

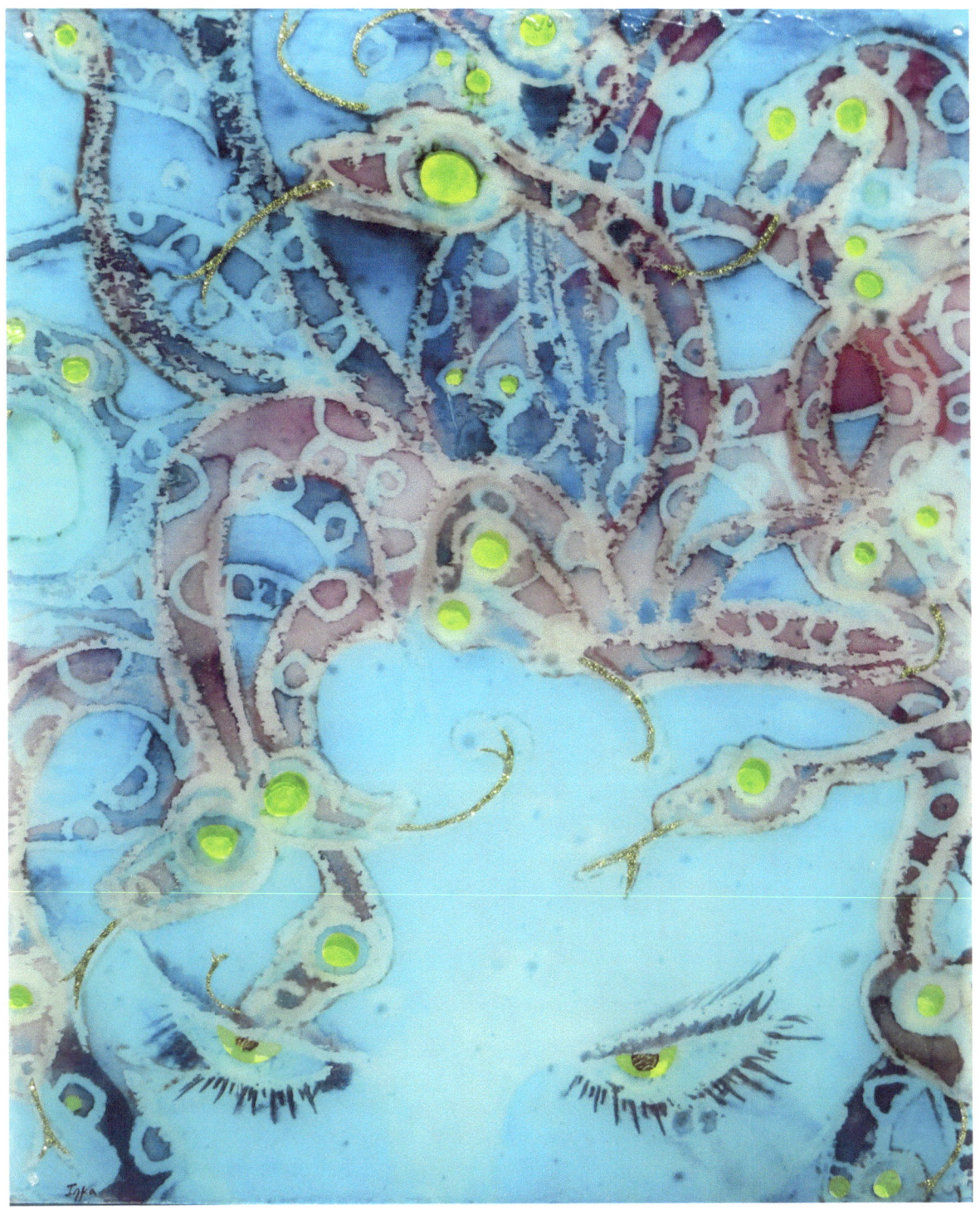

Gorgona Medusa

by Inna Timokhina, 2017, 100 cm x 80 cm,
Mixed Media on Plexiglass

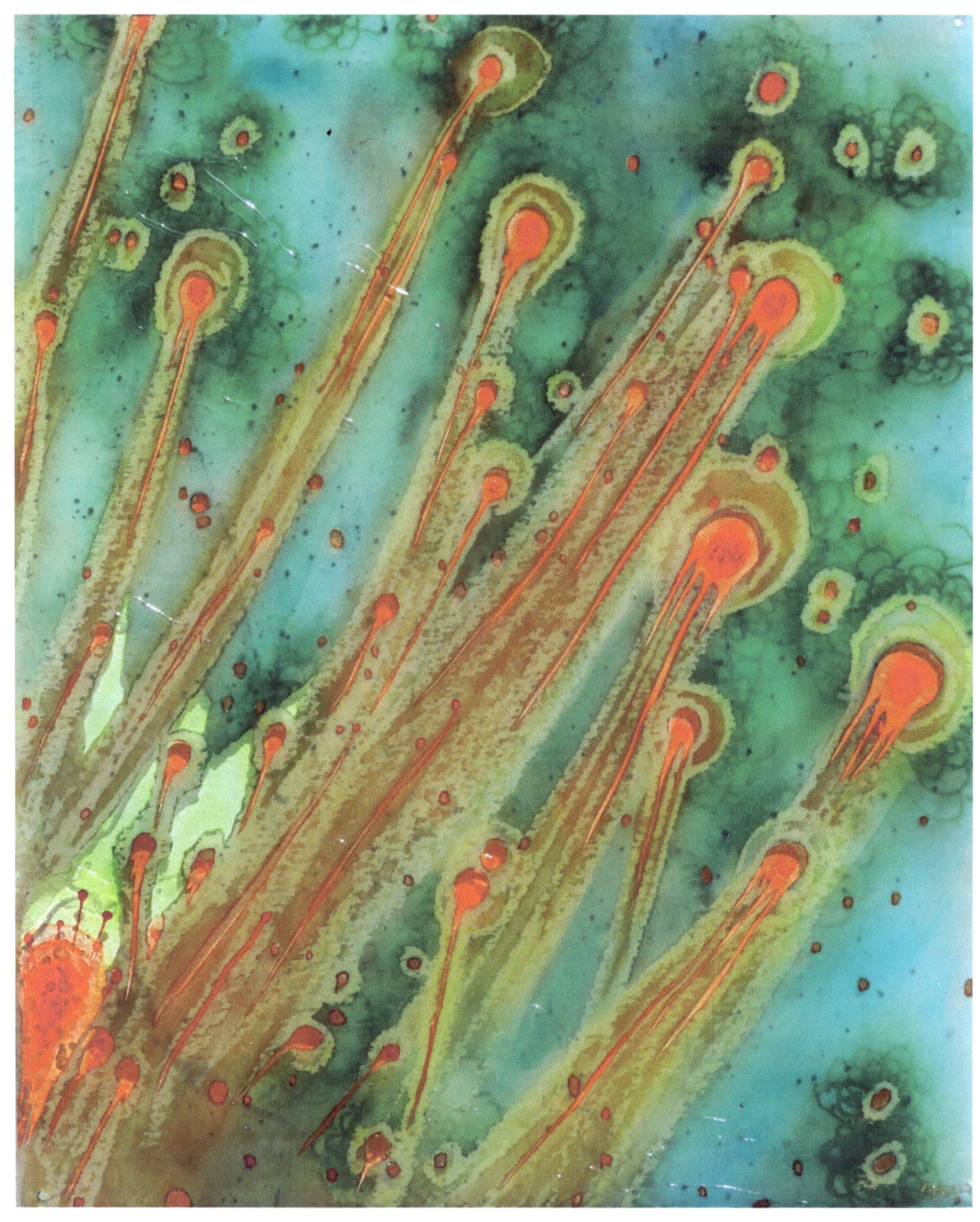

Acquamour

by Inna Timokhina, 2017, 100 cm x 80 cm,
Mixed Media on Plexiglass

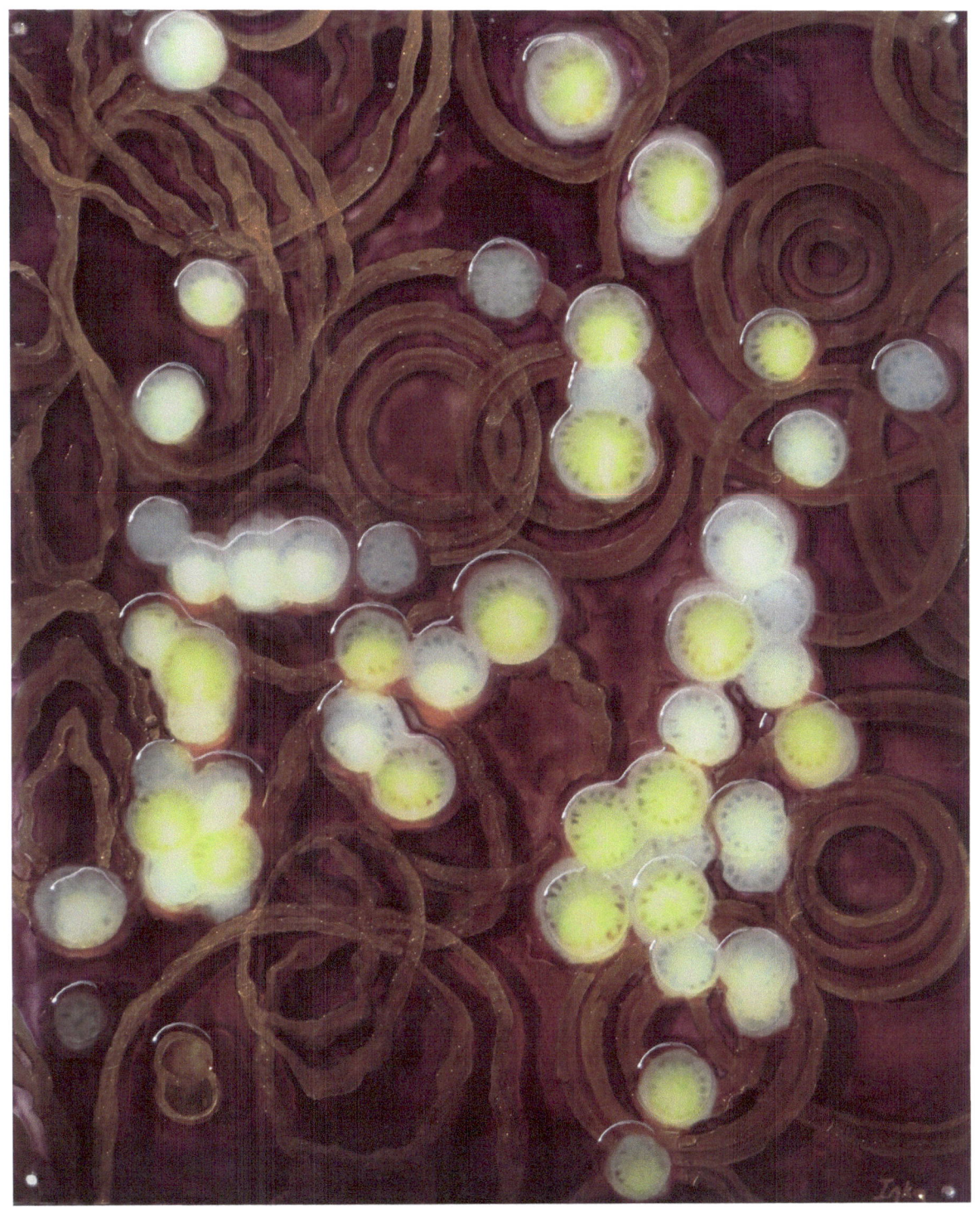

Cosmic Rendezvous

by Inna Timokhina, 2017, 100 cm x 80 cm,
Mixed Media on Plexiglass

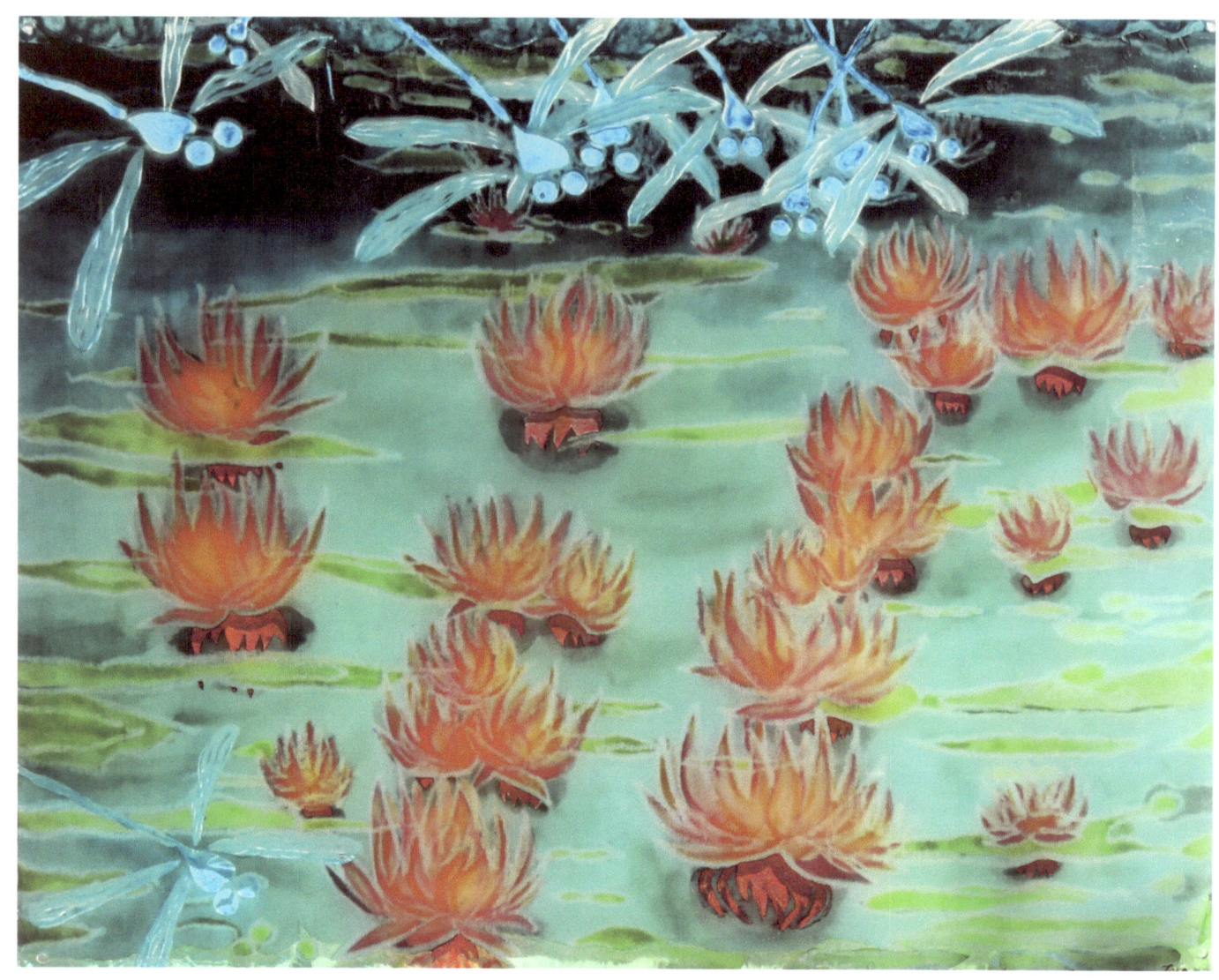

Fire Lotus

by Inna Timokhina, 2017, 100 cm x 80 cm,
Mixed Media on Plexiglass

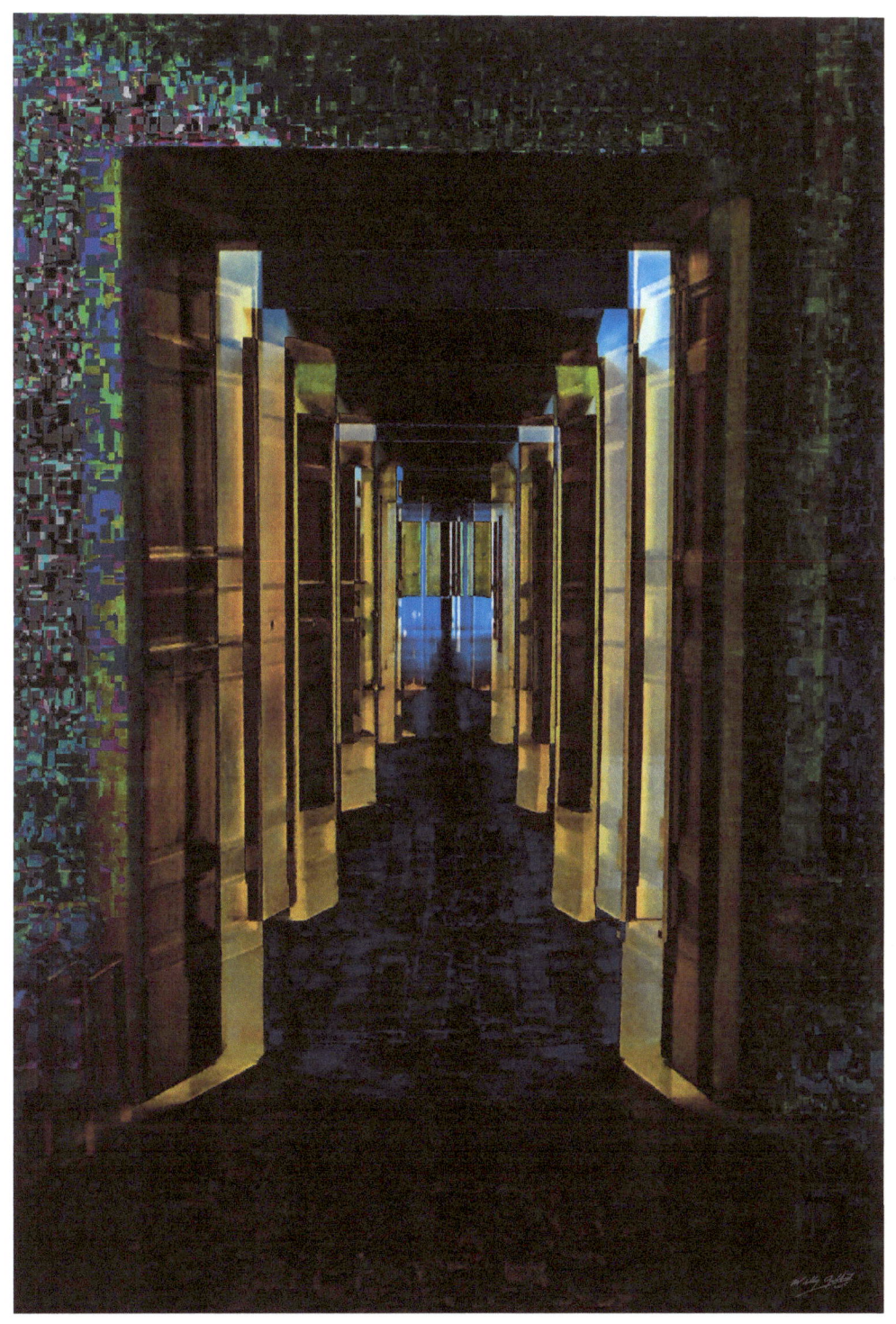

Doors to Nowhere

by Wally Gilbert, 2015, 152cm x 102cm,
Printed on Aluminum, edition of 5

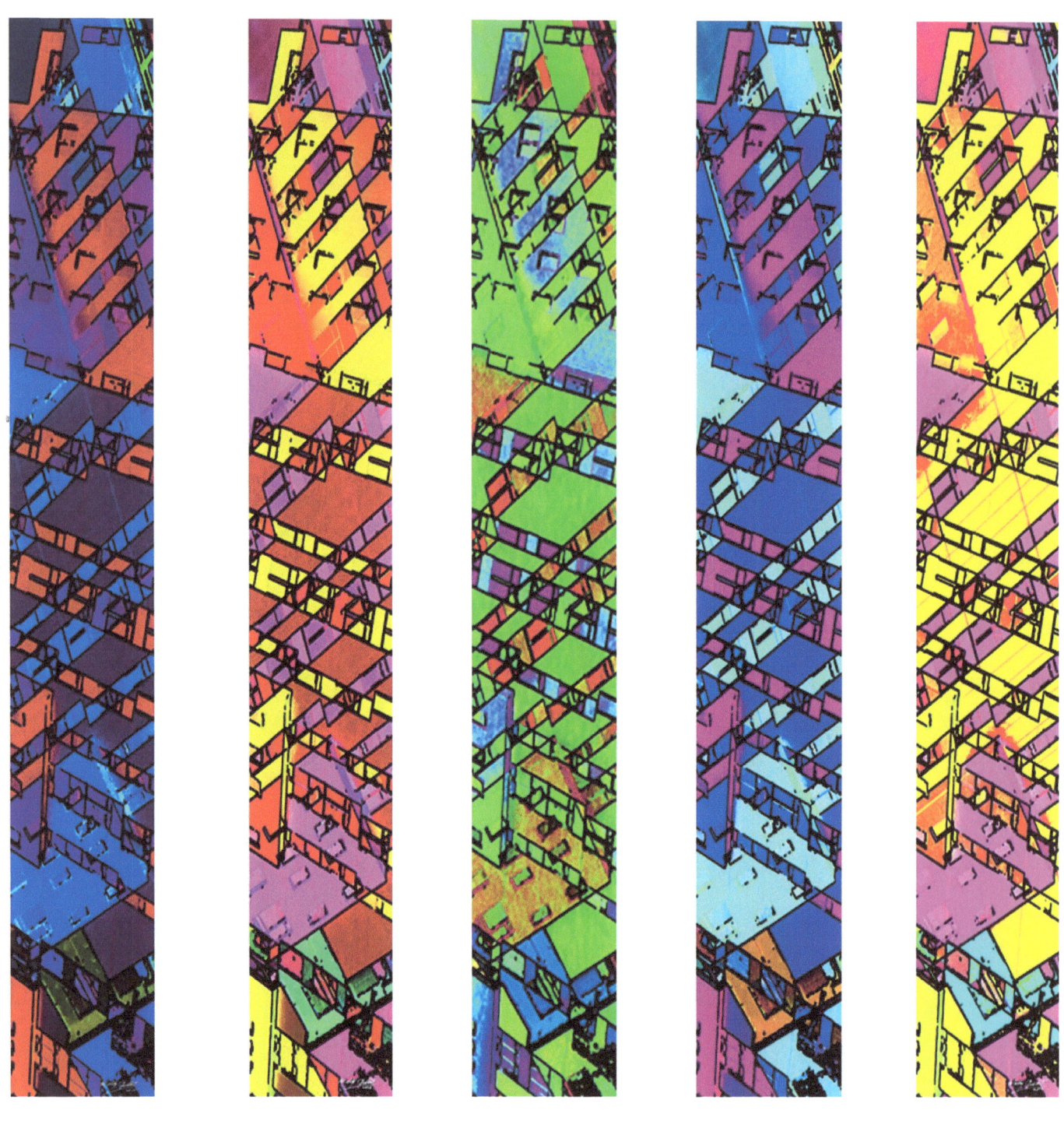

Torn Building Towers

by Wally Gilbert, 2016, Five Panels, each 183cm x 25cm,
Printed on Aluminum, edition of 5

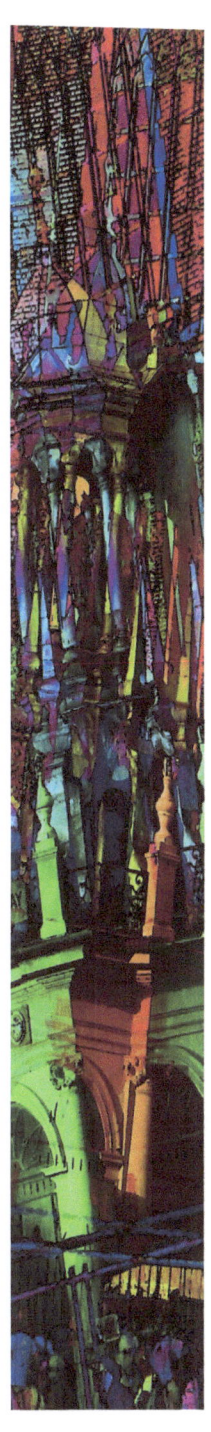

Youth Day – Krakow

by Wally Gilbert, 2016, 183cm x 25cm,
Printed on Aluminum, edition of 5

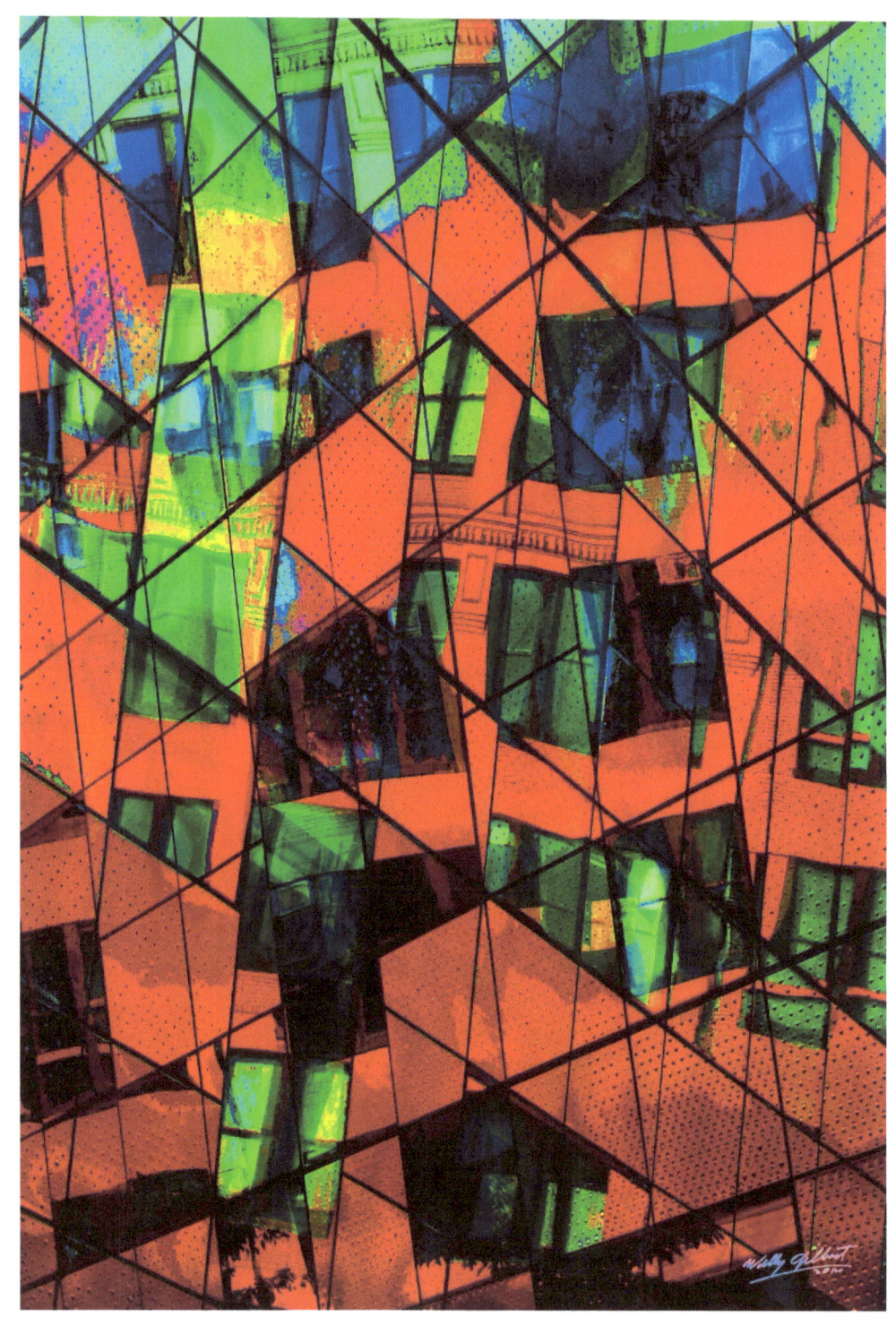

Broken City

by Wally Gilbert, 2014, 91cm x 61cm,
Printed on Aluminum, edition of 5

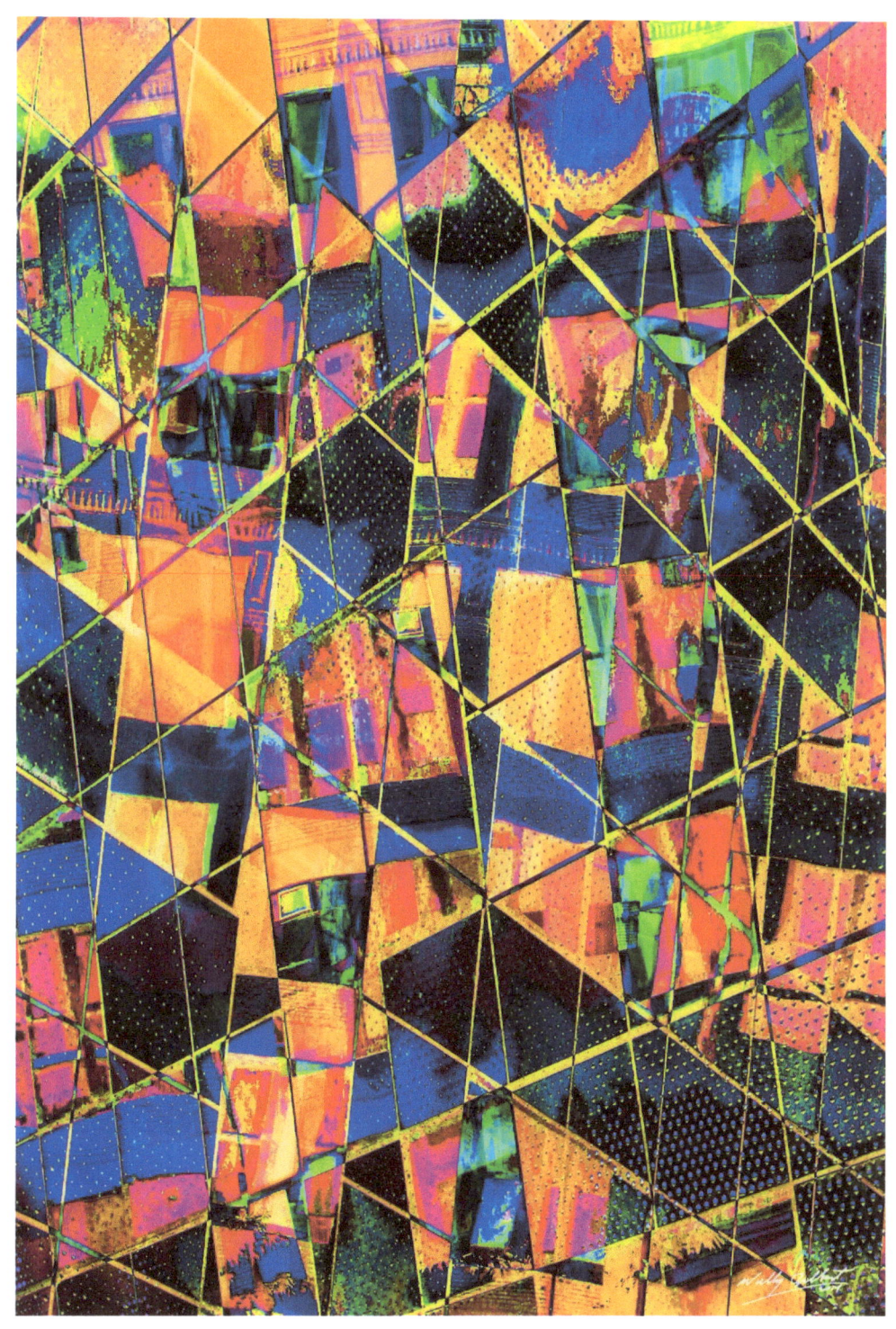

Broken City #II

by Wally Gilbert, 2014, 91cm x 61cm,
Printed on Aluminum, edition of 5

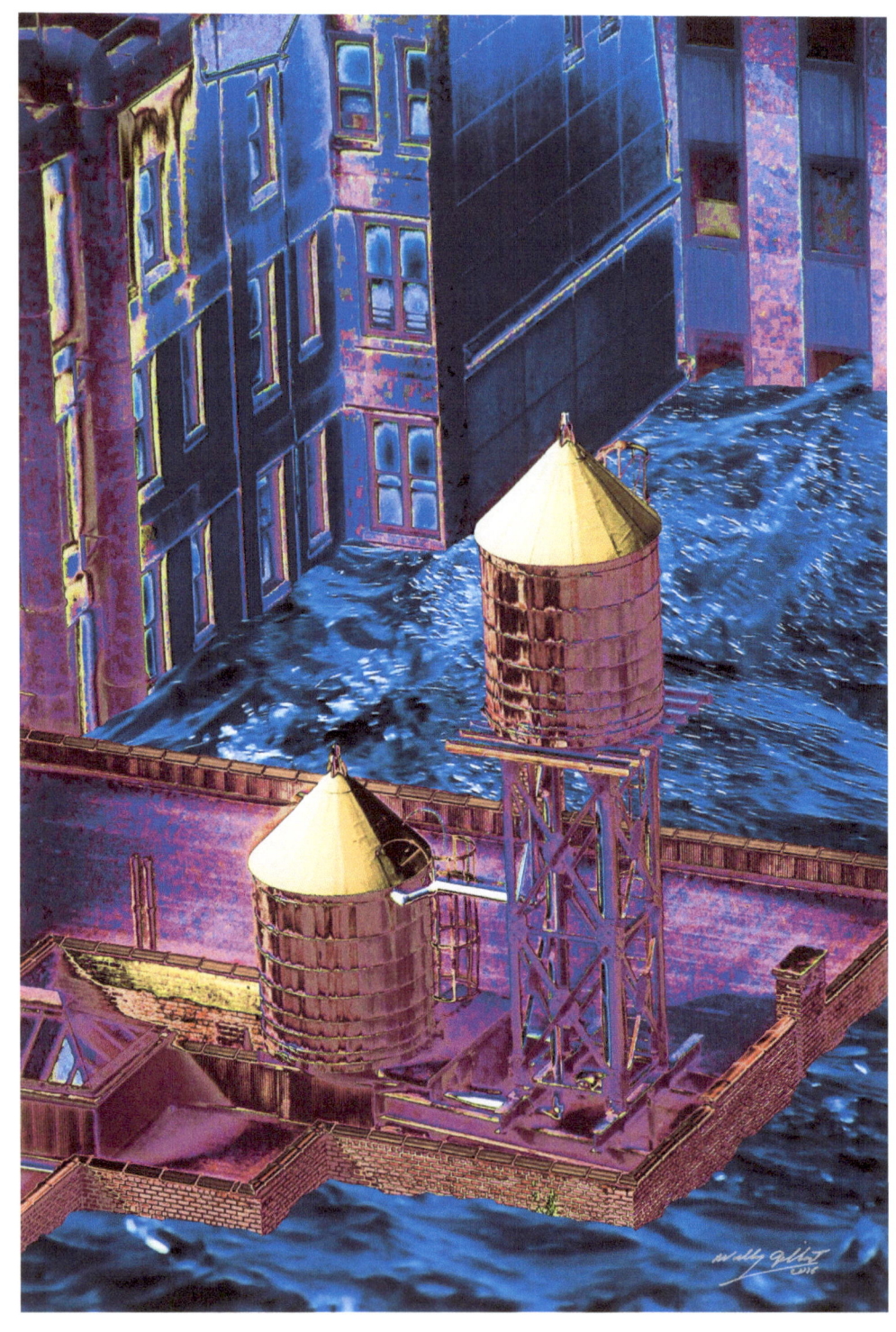

High Water – New York

by Wally Gilbert, 2016, 91cm x 61cm,
Printed on Aluminum, edition of 5

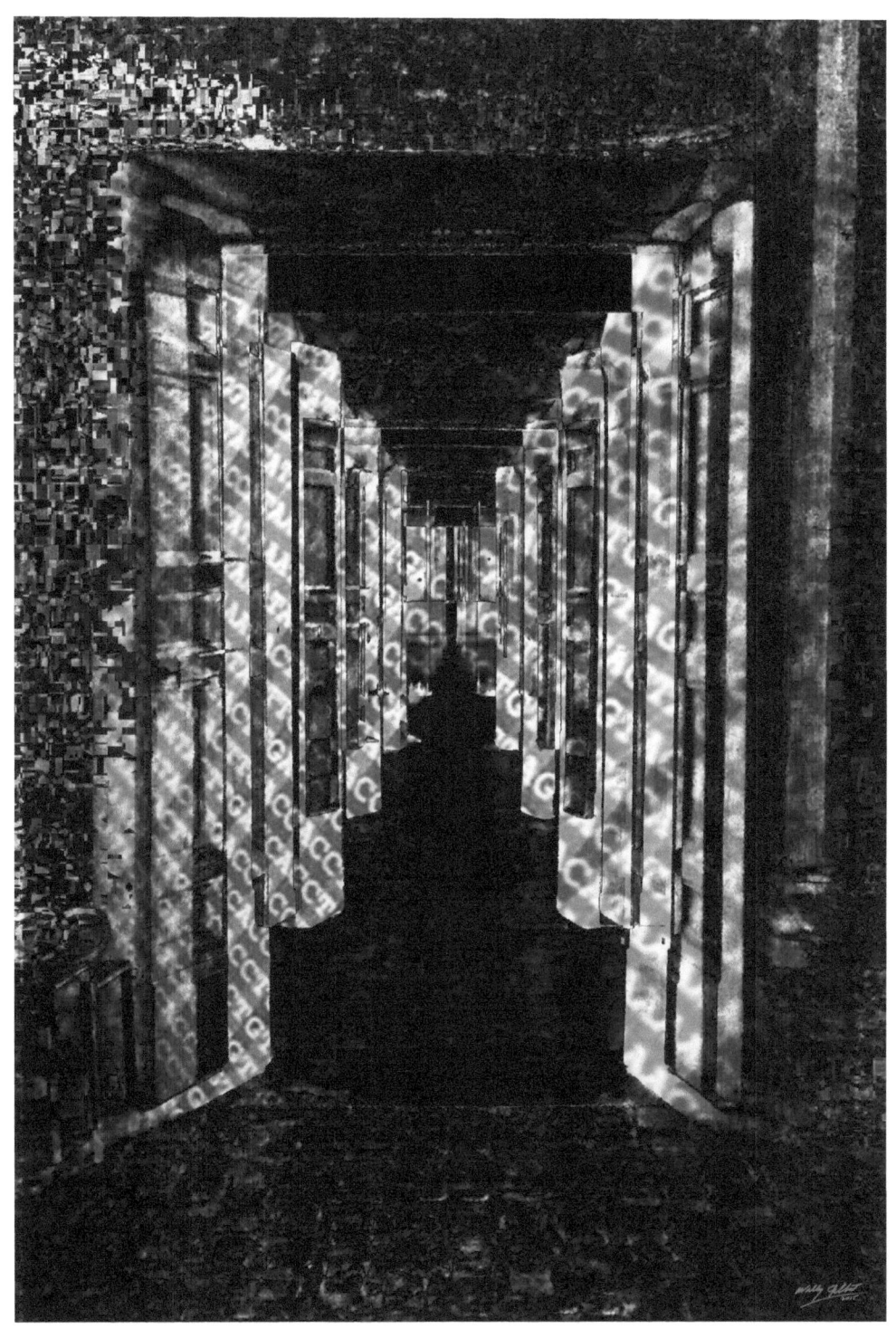

Sequences Forever

by Wally Gilbert, 2015, 76cm x 51cm,
Printed on Aluminum, edition of 5

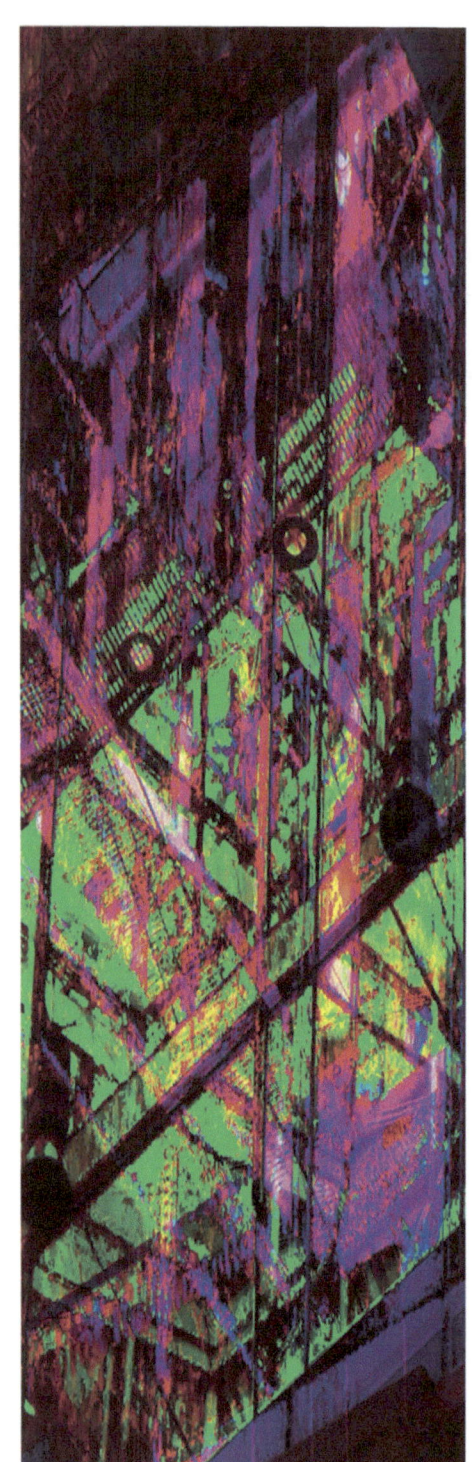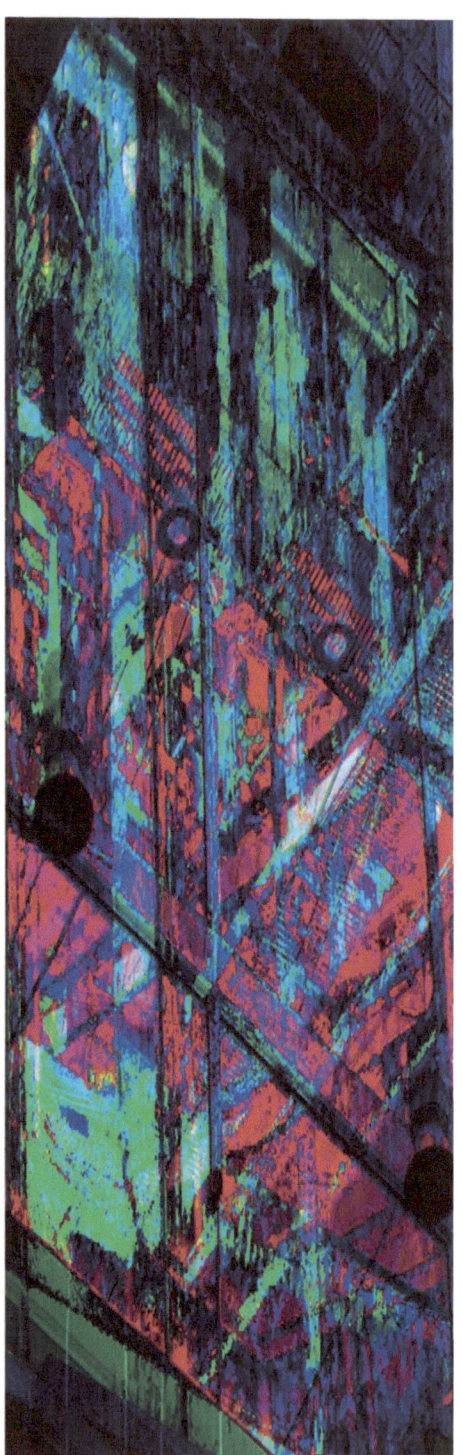

Multiply Diptych

by Wally Gilbert, 2016, Two Panels, each 91cm x 30cm,
Printed on Aluminum, edition of 5

Inna Timokhina

Inna Timokhina (aka INKA) is an international artist and a scientist, who spent her formative years in the New York City. She now lives and works in Zurich, Switzerland. She received a formal education in visual arts in Russia and a Ph.D. in Molecular Biology from Cornell University.

INKA's artistic work has been vividly described in an article that appeared in the Aesthetica Magazine in May 2014:

> "Mythical archetypes and molecular science find common ground in the work of Inna Timokhina, an artist-scientist with Siberian gypsy roots. INKA's art explores the hidden patterns and energies behind our familiar world, emerging from the viewpoints of microscopic and molecular images of life and from esoteric dreamworlds of the deep psyche. Using inspiration from her work as a molecular biologist, INKA's paintings depict unusual and dream-like scenes that appear to be in flux and evolving in unexpected and fantastic ways. As one of her collectors noted: 'Depending on the mood and the viewpoint of the viewer, INKA's paintings can trigger different and changing imaginations and emotions'.
>
> The energetic aspects of Inna's art, sometimes enhanced with actual light sources and at other times mimicking an 'infrared' point of view, like in night vision, contribute to this effect. This alternative interpretation of familiar images has created the notion of 'phantasmagoric dreamworld images'."

INKA developed a special technique that combines rare botanical inks, acrylics, epoxy resins, and other experimental materials on canvas, silk, or plexiglass. The space and energy effects of her paintings are often enhanced via illumination by custom made LED light circuits.

Artist's Statement

My main fascination in the artistic process is to capture, visualize, and amplify hidden energies behind human emotions, ideas, or states of mind. When these energies are revealed, they appear to be independent from gravity and have their own flow. Drawing from my background as a molecular scientist, I often approach artistic process as a magic experiment, where pure creativity is intertwined with scientific precision in amplifying energy. In my latest collection I combine ink on silk painting with plexiglass and layers of colored resins. This technique results in semitransparent dreamlike images, which also become 2.5 dimensional.

INKA's Artwork Inspirations.

"Space–Time." A constellation of powerful glowing energy spheres is pulling the viewer deeper and deeper into the parallel worlds.

"Pearls of Passion." Spheres, filled with glowing matter of passion are ascending through, and in spite of, a tight network of prejudice.

"Jazz me up!" Blue-orange sparkles of melody are in harmony with groovy-green circles of rhythm. "Jazz me up!" was inspired by the song from Swing Syndicate, influenced by cultural movements of London and New York in Electro Jazz.

"Gorgona Medusa." The powerful energy of Medusa is not of a violent nature, but is very focused on following her visions. She will only turn living creatures into stones if they create obstacles on her path. The image of Medusa is captured in a motion of raising up her eyes to meet the eyes of the viewer. Her hair-snakes are alert and constantly moving.

"Aquamour." An explosion of spheres, filled with glowing "elixir of love", is like an underwater geyser. The flying Aquamour spheres have perfectly directed energy momentums and are not going to miss their target.

"Cosmic Rendezvous." There is a cosmic rendezvous in a secret spacetime, and, as a result, a brilliant new idea is born.

"Fire Lotus." Red Lotus flowers are emerging from the pond and turning into the flames of passion. This pond is getting too hot for icy-blue dragonflies.

Inna Timokhina   Exhibitions

Solo Exhibitions:

2012	"The Dreamworld Art" at the Museum of the Russian Art (MORA), USA.
2011	"Guest Artist – Inna Timokhina" at the Art Gallery of Potomac, USA.

Selected Exhibitions:

2017	Affordable Art Fair Singapore, Spring edition
2017	PREMIER ART FAIR Hong Kong, China
2016	SCOPE Miami Beach, Miami FL USA
2016	"Gates of Paradise" Group Exhibition, Miami FL USA
2016	SCOPE Basel (Art Basel week) with Arte Ponte gallery, Basel, Switzerland.
2016	"Soyons fous, ne nous prenons pas au serieux" Exhibition-Competition at GemlucArt to raise funds for the fight against cancer. Monaco.
2015	"ART Monaco 2015" at Espace FONTVIEILLE. Monaco.
2015	"Affordable Art Fair" Milan, Italy.
2015	"Soi même". Exhibition-Competition at GemlucArt to raise funds for the fight against cancer. Monaco.
2015	"To feed the Planet; Energy for Life", group exhibition dedicated to Milano Expo 2015; at Spazio Tadini, Milano, Italy.
2015	"Restlessness", Cratere Creativo Exhibition-Competition, organized by dall'Associazione Vesuviani in Cammino. Villa Ruoppolo, Naples, Italy.
2015	"Fashion ART" Group Exhibition. Galerie Etienne de Causans; Paris, France
2015	Salon Art Carrousel du Louvre, Paris, France
2014	"Elle et Lui" Exhibition-Competition at GemlucArt to raise funds for the fight against cancer. Monaco.
2014	"Small Wonders Piccole Meraviglie". LINEA Spazio Arte Contemporanea. Firenze, Italy.
2014	ART 3F Mulhouse Art Fair at Parc Expo de Mulhouse, Mulhouse, France.
2014	"RED AND WHITE, the colors of Montecarlo" at Art Monaco, Grimaldi Forum, Monte Carlo, Monaco
2014	"JAZZ a Nice" Group exhibition dedicated to Jazz. Galleria Monteoliveto, Nice, France.
2014	"La 7eme ART" Group exhibition dedicated to the Cinema - de Festival di Cannes. Galleria Monteoliveto, Nice, France.
2013	IX Florence Biennale, Firenze, Italy
2013	Chianciano Biennale, Museo d'Arte di Chianciano Terme, Chianciano (SI) Italy. Recipient of Certificate for Artistic Merit.
2013	"ART-LIKE" Group exhibition at Articblue Gallery, Ibiza, Spain.
2013	"Action Force" Group exhibition at Espace Kameleon, Paris, France.

2013	ART.FAIR, Cologne, Germany.
2013	Art Monaco, at Grimaldi Forum, Monte Carlo, Monaco.
2013	Affordable Art Fair with Gagliardi Gallery, at Battersea Evolution, London, UK.
2013	London Biennale at Chelsea old Town Hall, London, UK.
2012	"A Journey Into A Contemporary Secret Garden " at Onishi Gallery, New York, USA
2012	"Transcending Physicality Through Matter" at Articblue Gallery, Ibiza, Spain.
2012	Chuck Jones Center for Creativity "The Red Dot Auction – Celebrating the Chuck Jones Centennial", Invited Artist; Costa Mesa, California, USA
2012	Parallax International Contemporary Art Fair (Art Basel Miami week), at Wynwood Convention Centre, Miami, FL.
2012	Parallax International Contemporary Art Fair, at Chelsea old Town Hall, London UK.
2011	"Mini Solos" at Touchstone Gallery, Washington, USA.
2011	Chuck Jones Center for Creativity "The Red Dot Auction", Invited Artist. Costa Mesa, CA USA
2011	"Views of the Orient" Contemporary Expressions of Asian-Pacific Art in a Global Culture at UBS Stamford Art Gallery, Connecticut, USA.
2011	RED DOT Miami (Art Basel Miami week). Wynwood Art District, Miami FL USA.
2011	ArtExpo New York, Solo Booth, Pier 94 on the Hudson River, New York, USA

Selected Interviews/ Art Publications:

2017	Press release in Huadong Art Magazine http://huadong.artron.net/20170227/n911308.html Press release in Artslant https://www.artslant.com/ew/events/show/439387-premier-art-fair-during-art-basel-hong-kong-week
2016	Press release in Artfix Daily http://www.artfixdaily.com/artwire/release/7611-the-gates-of-paradise Press release in Artslant http://www.artslant.com/mia/events/show/430605-the-gates-of-paradise
2015	Featured in Royal Monaco Magazine: ROYAL MONACO JULY N°24 http://www.royalmonaco.net/2015/06/inna-timokhina-artist-to-artmonaco-in-july.html
2014	Interview with Aesthetica Magazine. http://www.aestheticamagazine.com/blog/interview-artist-inna-timokhina/ Featured in Monaco Reporter "Gemluc Art Monaco – Art Suporting Health" https://monacoreporter.com/2014/10/25/gemlucart-monaco-art-supporting-health/ Interviews with the Artists "GemlucArt 2014" https://youtu.be/olAh3WESfqk Featured in Royal Monaco Magazine: ROYAL MONACO OCTOBRE/NOVEMBRE N°21
2011	Press release: Views of the Orient Contemporary Expressions of Asian-Pacific Art in a Global Culture, *Asian Pacific Heritage Month Art Exhibition.* UBS Stamford Art Gallery. Potomac Almanac: Art Gallery Spotlights Timokhina and Spak. Potomac Patch: Two Artists Envision Unique Perspectives.

Wally Gilbert's Statement

I began making digital images as art when I discovered that I could make large prints from images taken with a small digital camera and that these prints carried an emotional and asthetic impact. My earliest work was of fragments of the visual world, either portions of natural scenes or of man's architectural or industrial artifacts. My first one-person show included a 48" x 72" image made from a two mega-pixel camera.

I was invited to Poland, to do an installation at the Norblin Site in Warsaw, by Jan Kubasiewicz and Josef Piwkowski. These photographs of decaying machinery were installed in Warsaw in the Summer of 2007 as twenty-six 12' x 8' hangings and thirty 36" x 24" prints, face-mounted on plexiglas. This show was exhibited again in Lodz and in Poznan.

After photographing dancers in the ballet, I went on to explore abstractions, first in a "Vanishing" series, that was based on a natural form, the outline of a human head. The many patterns produced in that series all shared some aspect of a biological or natural curve, which still was manifest even in the smallest cropping of those images.

In my later work the basic element was a straight, shaded line, which I used to create geometric patterns. The "Geometric Series" explored patterns in color or black-and-white created from overlapping squares or triangles or just from lines, taken either simply or in intersecting groups.

I make many images by hand on the computer. The computer simply holds the intermediate forms as I superpose the many layers I create to build up the image. The images begin in black and white, and then I color them in the computer. I generate these colors either by accessing the colors available or, in a more complicated fashion, by using the ability to change the global input-output functions for each color and intensity separately. When the layers containing the colored images interact with each other, still more color patterns appear. The computer is a digital workspace, driven by my hand and eye.

My most recent work involves photographs moved to extreme values in color space yielding strange color contrasts further superimposed on eachother. These images exemplify my delight in light and form, and my search for a three-dimensional effect on a two-dimensional surface. I search for depth beyond the picture plane and for mystery.

Wally Gilbert's Biography

Wally Gilbert had a long international career as a scientist, working in Molecular Biology on genes and DNA. He was awarded a Nobel Prize in Chemistry, in 1980, for solving the mystery of DNA sequencing. Fred Sanger in England and Gilbert in the United States shared that prize for finding ways to decipher the order of chemical groups along the DNA molecule and hence to make it possible for the first time to read the genes. Those discoveries drove the development of Biology as a gene-based science across the last four decades and led to the working out of the Human Genome program and the current understanding of all organisms.

For the last fifteen years Gilbert has been working in Digital Art. He began by making large images of fragments of the world, focusing on form, texture, and color, using a small digital camera. Very often these pictures were drawn from machines or from architecture. Jan Kubasiewicz, a professor at the Massachusetts College of Art, saw his work and organized his first one-person exhibition in 2004. He was invited to Poland, by Kubasiewicz and Jozef Zuk Piwkowski, to create an installation at the Norblin Site in Warsaw, an old decaying factory. This installation, consisting of twenty-six 12' by 8' hangings and thirty 36" x 24" prints face-mounted on Plexiglas, was installed at Norblin in Warsaw for two months in 2007 and then later that year in Łodz and again in Poznan in 2009. The set of thirty face-mounted prints were also exhibited in New York, Washington D.C., Los Angeles, and San Diego.

Gilbert was invited to participate in creating a book on the Boston Ballet Company. He spent several years photographing ballet dancers in rehearsal. These pictures, which capture the joy and motion of the dancers, appeared in a book on that company "Behind the Scenes at Boston Ballet" by Christine Temin with 68 pictures by Wally Gilbert.

Gilbert then moved to abstractions, first based on silhouettes derived from photographs, then to ever more abstract images based on the human head, at first still interpretable, but then in patterns having only a slight, residual aspect of a biological curve. Then he created digital images, made by hand on the computer, based on geometrical forms. This work involved patterns of superimposed shrinking squares and triangles, strongly colored or in black and white, and led finally to images involving single lines. More recently he has been exploring abstractions created by superimposing several photographic images.

Wally Gilbert — Selected Solo Exhibitions

"Towers" Viridian Gallery, Chelsea, NYC	2017
"Doors to Nowhere,' Salon R, Cambridge, MA	2017
"Broken City," Khaki Gallery, Boston, MA	2016
"Broken City" Viridian Gallery, Chelsea, NYC	2016
"Patterns & Recognition," Seoul National University Bundang Hospital, curated by Chang and Jae Kim	2015-2016
"Transformations," Viridian Artists, Chelsea, NYC	2014
"Patterns & Recognition," The Howard Hughes Medical Institure, Janelia Farm, VA	2014
"Wally Gilbert," CJ Gallery, Art San Diego 2013, San Diego, CA	2013
"Wally Gilbert: A Room of Light," Milton Art Museum, Canton, MA	2013
"Wally Gilbert: Black & White," Khaki Gallery, Boston, MA	2013
"Digital Constellations," Lindau City Museum, Lindau, Germany	2013
"Wally Gilbert: New Black and White Images," Viridian Artists, Chelsea, NYC	2013
"Wally Gilbert", CJ Gallery, Art San Diego 2012, San Diego, CA	2012
"En-Lighten," Khaki Gallery, Boston, MA	2012
"Journeying," The Artemis Gallery, Krakow, Poland, curated by Wieslawa Piotrowska-Sowadska	2012
"Pattern & Recognition," The Art Gallery, Antelope Valley College, Lancaster, CA	2012
"Squares, Triangles, and Lines," Galerie im Einstein, Berlin	2011
"Projekt Norblin," New Art Wet Music Foundation, Bydgoszcz, Poland	2011
"Squares and Triangles," Viridian Artists, Chelsea, NYC	2011
"Vanishing," CJ Gallery, San Diego, CA	2010
"Vanishing Profiles," Khaki Gallery, Boston, MA	2010
"The Norblin Project and Other Images," CJ Gallery and OCIO DESIGN GROUP, San Diego,CA	2010
"Wally@Wainwright," Wainwright Bank, Cambridge, MA	2010
"Vanishing," BAAK Gallery, Cambridge, MA	2009
Norblin Installation, Poznan, Poland, curated by Jan Kubasiewicz and Zuk Piwkowski	2009
"The Norblin Project and other Images," CJ Art Gallery, San Diego, CA	2009
"IN COLOR & BEYOND," Khaki Gallery, Boston, MA	2009
"Fresh Fruit," Mayyim Hayyim Gallery, Newton, MA	2009
"Stillness and Motion," Viridian Artists, Chelsea, NYC	2008
"LEEKS & CHAINS," Khaki Gallery, Wellesley, MA	2008
"The Norblin Project and other Images," CJ Art Gallery, San Diego, CA	2007
BAAK Gallery, Cambridge, MA	2007
Norblin Installation, Galeria PATIO,Lodz, Poland, curated by Zuk Piwkowski, Jan Kubasiewicz, and Aurelia Mandziuk	2007
Norblin Site Installation, Warsaw, Poland, curated by Jan Kubasiewicz and Zuk Piwkowski	2007
"The Norblin Project: Images of Decay," American Center for Physics, College Park, MD	2007
"IN COLOR," Khaki Gallery, Wellesley, MA	2007
"The Norblin Project: Images of Decay," LACDA, Los Angeles, CA	2006
"The Norblin Project: Images of Decay," Viridian Artists, Chelsea, NYC	2006
Jock Colville Hall, Churchill College, University of Cambridge, Cambridge, UK	2006
Ann Janss Gallery, Los Angeles, CA	2005
Doran Gallery, Massachusetts College of Art, Boston, MA, curated by Jan Kubasiewicz	2004

www.ingramcontent.com/pod-product-compliance
Lightning Source LLC
Chambersburg PA
CBHW051819210526
45473CB00005B/1670